OUR
LADY
of the
RUINS

Our Lady of the Ruins is poetry for the new century: awake to the world, spiritually profound, and radiant with intelligence. It is also a visionary work, wherein the poet recognizes the urgencies of our post-apocalyptic present, for she is standing, as the stone lady stood in the ruins of bombed Dresden (as it happens, near the Church of Our Lady), keeping vigil in the aftermath, and echoing Walter Benjamin's angel whose back is turned to the chaos blown skyward, so as to hold open the possibility of denying oblivion its dominion. In Brimhall's near-surreal language, we are invited to imagine a world half ended and half continuing, a world our own and almost recognizable to us. It is an unsettling recognition, and it is the poet's achievement that she brings us to where we are *unharmed / but not safe*. Here is a signature passage, from "Diaspora": *You know your way by the wreckage, // by torches and dust, by the watermark / on walls where floods reached to touch / the fading portraits. Ghosts refuse // to abandon the ruins. They deliver no message / but the past. Don't enter the river, they say. / Don't trust the dream that wakes you.* This is the realm of the prophetic, which does not suggest a gift for reading the future, but rather for perceiving what the present will become. We are here, where there are *minnows / swimming in the drowned girl's lungs* and *deer licking salt from a lynched man's palm*. Old myths and faiths do not help us, as *the graveyard is full of dead prophets*, and not even madness offers a way out, as *no one believes in madness anymore*. The poet Brimhall recognizes that in our time, perhaps *It isn't even God we're looking for. // We want to ride the horse of the past backward.* There are many such insights among these prayers, nocturnes, hymns, and requia, and there is also something else, as uncommon as is Brimhall's visionary sensibility, and that is her *answering silence*, an active silence that suffuses this extraordinary collection, and accompanies us to the end.

—Carolyn Forché

OUR
LADY
of the
RUINS

Traci Brimhall

W. W. NORTON & COMPANY

NEW YORK · LONDON

For information about permission to reproduce selections from this book,
write to Permissions, W. W. Norton & Company, Inc.,
500 Fifth Avenue, New York, NY 10110

For information about special discounts for bulk purchases, please contact W. W. Norton
Special Sales at specialsales@wwnorton.com or 800-233-4830

Manufacturing by Courier Westford
Book design by Joanne Metsch
Production manager: Louise Mattarelliano

Library of Congress Cataloging-in-Publication Data

Brimhall, Traci, 1982–
Our lady of the ruins / Traci Brimhall. — 1st ed.
p. cm.
ISBN 978-0-393-08643-0 (pbk.)
I. Title.
PS3602.R53177O97 2012
811'.6—dc23

2011040073

W. W. Norton & Company, Inc.
500 Fifth Avenue, New York, N.Y. 10110
www.wwnorton.com

W. W. Norton & Company Ltd.
Castle House, 75/76 Wells Street, London W1T 3QT

1 2 3 4 5 6 7 8 9 0

The demon that you can swallow gives you its power.

—Joseph Campbell

Contents

Acknowledgments

Many thanks to the editors of the following publications where these poems first appeared, sometimes in earlier versions:

Beloit Poetry Journal: "Come Trembling" & "The Orchard of Infinite Pears"

Blackbird: "Our Lady of the Ruins," "Sans Terre," & "To Poison the Lion"

Copper Nickel: "The Needful Animal" & "Our Bodies Break Light"

Diode: "Hysteria: A Requiem"

Epiphany: "The Cities That Sleep"

Field: "A Year Between Wars" (October)

Indiana Review: "Petition" & "Prayer to the Deaf Madonna"

iO: "The Blessing" & "The Visitation"

Iron Horse Literary Review: "How to Find the Underworld"

Jai-Alai Magazine: "Inheritance"

The Journal: "Parable of the Cannibals" & "Parable of Love's Twelve Apostles"

Kenyon Review Online: "The Sunken Gospel"

Linebreak: "The Colossus"

Memorious: "Requiem for the First Born"

Mid-American Review: "Exodus" & "Pilgrimage"

New England Review: "Envoi" & "Somniloquy"

New South: "Auto-da-Fé," "Late Novena," & "Winter Nocturne"

Ninth Letter: "To My Unborn Daughter"

Parthenon West Review: "Gnostic Fugue" & "Stillborn Elegy"

Quarterly West: "Become the Lion" & "The New World"

Third Coast: "Dirge for the Idol"

Virginia Quarterly Review: "Prelude to a Revolution"

Washington Square Review: "The Revisionist Gospel"

I am deeply indebted to people whose insights and feedback helped shape the manuscript: Adam Clay, Gillian Cummings, Elizabyth Hiscox, Douglas Jones, Robert McCowen, Gary McDowell, Martin Rock, Brynn Saito, Anne Shaw, and Chad Sweeney.

I am also grateful to Nancy, Claudia, Tricia, Jill, Krystal, Bronwen, Matthew, Melissa, and Christine who always keep me writing and who looked at numerous poems in their early stages.

I would also like to thank the English Department at Western Michigan University for their support, Carolyn Forché for her faith in this manuscript, and Jill Bialosky and everyone at W. W. Norton who helped make this book possible.

OUR
LADY
of the
RUINS

Music from a Burning Piano

Imagine half the world ends and the other half continues
in a city made holy by pilgrims who wander to it.

They stare at a saint's hand in the reliquary, unchanged.
Every day the same parade of radiance and crows.

Every day thirsting for edible gods. Priests lie well
enough to save their own lives. Yes, everything is alive

but not equally loved. Imagine children are named
the new historians. Streets forget the revolution.

Imagine a piano lit on fire and pushed off a roof.
Music falls past windows, but it never meets its shadow.

We know it disappeared by the generation of silence.
When we visit wild acres and return, the sky moves

beneath our skin. Prison guards brand execution dates
onto condemned bodies, reminding flesh what the brain

relinquished, a century in an hourglass, skin a scaffolding
of cells. It's not how much you suffer, but where.

Prisoners peel new scabs and watch travelers arrive from
a vanishing road, listen for hammers striking burning strings.

Prelude to a Revolution

We go to prison windows and pass cigarettes, tangerines
and iodine through the bars. Anything we think

could heal a man. Assassins kiss our fingers.
Mercenaries sing us songs about unbroken light

as we mend their shirts. The bilingual murderers recite
lamentations in one tongue, and in another, young myths.

We fold and unfold our shawls, and the men squint
into the sunlight, dumb with hope. Some days they confuse

the walls of their cage with their skin. Some days,
the sky. They see their deaths in the sweat darkening

our dresses. To sweeten the hours we share scandals
from the city, how curators removed an elephant's heart

from the museum because it began beating when anyone
in love looked at it, how the coroner found minnows

swimming in a drowned girl's lungs. They ask if it's true,
if slaves are chained together on ships to prevent suicide.

We say they'll never be free. They warn us one night soon
the judge will wake to find his bed alive with wasps,

while across town the night watchman will stare stunned
at the moths circling before he realizes he's on fire.

Prayer to the Deaf Madonna

Once, I was a mystery unto myself,
but desire and hunger taught me
about my body. Once, I held the head

of an oracle over a fire to hear her speak.
She cried, *Blood oranges! Birds of paradise!*
But I'd burned the soldiers and buried

the armor. I heard a sword humming
in its sheath. I heard my voice behind
the mirror, a child's first lie, the clock

marking out quantities of darkness.
Yes, I profited from war. My children lived.
They ate apricots and honey. And it's true—

when I found the mandrake growing beneath
the feet of the garroted man, I ate it.
It tasted like a libertine's semen and sweat,

but it made my heart a safe place for music.
Help me forget my trespasses and the way rain
hides itself in everything it touches.

I will not give the night what it wants.
No cursing yellow moons. No proud surrender.
I have to disguise fugitives, to wrap the dead

in flags, to bring the wounded water
and a priest, and I have my country,
I have my country to fear.

A Year Between Wars

January
The road offers itself to us, but rocks below cut light into
shadows. Everywhere we travel signs say: *Do not disturb the prayers tied
to trees*, but the branches are empty.

February
We wipe snow from the sundial and tell a cardinal in the frozen
fountain about women dancing in basements during the raids.
We tell frostbitten grass about girls who traded their bodies to
soldiers for bread.

March
The priests banish the words *home, wind, desire.*

April
Each week we build a new god and take the ashes of yesterday's
god to the sea.

May
Spring returns with its terrible resurrection. Our mother skins
the bull she loves and makes us all coats.

June
One book sentences another to burning. One language sleeps to
keep the world at a distance. The bees interview new flowers.

July
A pregnant woman drowns herself in a well. No one drinks from
it now. We wander from the city walls to the river. Cormorants
dive for the silver flash of fish and then surface.

August
A deaf man paints the tombstones blue because he can't hear
his own prayers. Forgiveness does not release him. Even though
he asks for it. For the way he used the body offered to him,
and what he did with the body he paid for. One was weary and
splendor-worn. One was the shadow of heaven.

September
Weeks pass and the sky stays quiet. We are braver and more
afraid.

October
We steal the hand from the reliquary to find the miracle and
unmake it, to untie the hair it plaited, to restore the infant's fever.
We rave. We tantalize. We save the flood for another world.

November
We enter the river for the spellbinding. Somewhere between what
we say and what we hide, lies the word made flesh.

December
Old soldiers prophesy the new war. We build the walls higher.
We lock the gates. The flies gathering on our lips are bringing us
fruit.

The Labyrinth

We pay to walk the labyrinth on the cathedral floor,
to enter the circle and be changed. Humming

unwritten hymns, we rehearse the story to resurrect
the truth. Every canticle is an absolution.

Every requiem a gift for the God we made in the image
of our father. The madonnas shiver in the nascent dark

of their robes. They warn us: *you must trust what is sacred
inside you, or endure it,* and continue their patient

ministry of birds who will not be consoled, who repeat
the horrors they saw in the gargoyles' mouths.

No, the abyss isn't infinite. A half-light lurks even there.
We hold still to learn eternity and feel snow drift

from holes in the roof. We swear to be good, to love
our mothers, but even when we lie to God,

he listens. The walls whistle their low warning.
Wind sings through bullet holes in the windows.

The Visitation

In the new dream, we search for a sacrifice,
put our fingers in our own wounds,

wake with our hands over each other's mouths.
Boys return from war as men who know

two languages. We learn three so we will know
the message when we hear it. The street prophet

says, *If God is your enemy, rejoice, for the darkness*
remembers you. In the old dream, we readied

our stainless altar, but a wolf stole our offering.
We were lucky enough to sing the song once,

but we couldn't bring the dead any joy. Men ask
to borrow our sadness so they won't have to feel

their own. *Yes,* we say and kissed their arms. Yes, trees
cover us with shadows. We give the prophet money

to save something we'll never see. In the first dream,
men accept a new ecstasy. Our breath shows itself

to us and disappears. As we enter the woods,
the astonished wolf lifts its mouth from the lamb.

Diaspora

Wait. If you brush the pollen from your cheek,
you'll startle the heron in the reeds.
This is not the place your life begins or ends.

It is where cranes teach their colts to fear
what does not fly, where hornets feed
on fallen pears while you watch a swallowtail

test its new wings over the berm,
unused to its second life. You are unharmed
but not safe. You, chosen for your doubt,

remain on the bridge, caught in your quiet
passage from one broken country to another.
You know your way by the wreckage,

by torches and dust, by the watermark
on walls where floods reached to touch
the fading portraits. Ghosts refuse

to abandon the ruins. They deliver no message
but the past. Don't enter the river, they say.
Don't trust the dream that wakes you.

Our Bodies Break Light

We crawl through the tall grass and idle light,
our chests against the earth so we can hear the river

underground. Our backs carry rotting wood and books
that hold no stories of damnation or miracles.

One day as we listen for water, we find a beekeeper—
one eye pearled by a cataract, the other cut out by his own hand

so he might know both types of blindness. When we stand
in front of him, he says we are prisms breaking light into color—

our right shoulders red, our left hips a wavering indigo.
His apiaries are empty except for dead queens, and he sits

on his quiet boxes humming as he licks honey from the bodies
of drones. He tells me he smelled my southern skin for miles,

says the graveyard is full of dead prophets. To you, he presents
his arms, tattooed with songs slave catchers whistle

as they unleash the dogs. He lets you see the burns on his chest
from the time he set fire to boats and pushed them out to sea.

You ask why no one believes in madness anymore,
and he tells you stars need a darkness to see themselves by.

When you ask about resurrection, he says, *How can you doubt?*
and shows you a deer licking salt from a lynched man's palm.

Pilgrimage

Signs on the trees say it is forbidden
to take your life in the woods,
but people sway from branches,

swords rust between their ribs.
The grass repeats its eternal rumor
that everything which dies grows

a new body. We are faithful pilgrims
seeking your unfaithful hand, trying
to journey farther than our doubt,

to return to you the way all light
wants to return to fire rather than
travel from it. *Unto us a forest is born,*

we recite from the book where it is written
that you so loved the world you disguised
yourself as a hawk and also as the arrow

in its breast. As a fawn, and the ticks
feeding upon it. As a child's cry
in the night and the answering silence.

The Cities That Sleep

When we are lost, we unbutton her dress
and bend her over. She holds her ankles,
loving her helplessness as we orient ourselves

by the map inked into her back. We trace
the river winding down her spine, widening
with age as we search for roads that will take us

to their promised ends. We name unseen
oceans on her breasts and the cities that sleep
under our fingers, recite mountain ranges

and the elegies we have begun writing for each other.
We know the journey to God is a fatal one.
It isn't even God we're looking for.

We want to ride the horse of the past backward
through time to first wounds, laughter and milk,
but instead we drink from the beginnings of rivers.

Instead, I take the needle from the fire. I burn the day's
wanderings into her back. She whimpers with pleasure.
Only when I hurt her do I know she will stay.

How to Read a Compass

Take the blackbirds from your hair and lay them in the grass. If
   their eggs hatch in your hands, go north.

Take the web from the dead magician's mouth. If a spider crawls
   out, head south.

Take the gold from your neighbor's river and throw it at the
   stained-glass hymn. The words that don't break are a message.

Take the marchers to the forbidden monument.

Take the impatient minutes to the mountain.

Find a betrayer in a tree. Take the silver from his pockets.

Find the village besieged by war where the monk set himself on
   fire in protest. Find the immaculate muscle which did not
   burn, and take it.

Exodus

They are coming. All of them, with bouquets
of embers arousing their dull flesh as sinners sing
apples off the trees. There's nothing left to offer

except their stolen lamentations and the children
they buried without names. A monk confesses
he met two angels, wrestled twice, lost both

to the morning. A butcher warns, *The soldiers*
died and now the gods rise wearing armor.
But the midwife says, *We serve by suffering.*

Out of the tent, the penitents crawl low enough
to the ground to hear the fire at its core murmur,
Follow your shadow. It leads to your past.

Two by two, they climb the hill in original silence,
tongues swollen by everything they do not say.
The kingdom of ruin is within them—

the meteorite, the fever, the pharaoh's first born.
They open their robes, revealing the wounds
they made so love could enter, but what arrives

on the wind is pollen and dirt. From the statue's arms
libelous crows watch them stagger into their second life,
bent by rapture. Theirs is the freedom of the bound.

Bound to the season's cycles, to lavender
and hornets. Bound to the wheel that turns and turns
and never lifts them whole from the waiting earth.

The Colossus

In the beginning, none of us could tell rock
from bone. Some claim the desert was once a sea,
and the statue we found facedown in the sand

was a god who hardened as the waters dried.
Others say raiders stole it from an imperial city
but buried it when they discovered its curse.

Each morning we welcome bodies
from under the giant and reassemble them
in postures of praise. The colossus daily releases

the fossilized disciples beneath it, but the revelation
of stone is slow. Our mallets grow worn, our dowels
dull. The earth falls away, and still it hides

its face from us. We sleep on its back, dance
on its neck, and in sandstorms we crawl beneath
its hands and pray the wind won't take us.

We measure the width of its shoulders, take the radius
of its bald heels, wind ropes around its shoulders,
winch it to a wheel, but none of us turns the handle

to raise it. What if we recognize the face? What if
the world doesn't end here? Everything will come true—
the flood, the famine, the miracle.

The Needful Animal

Say the body is a door. Say pain invites me
to a darkness where I am the only guest.

Say a new battlefield is lit by strange flames
living over the dead. I hold out a knife to beguile

the light, but it isn't fooled. It leads me deeper
into my lostness, to the place where stars go

to sleep and wind goes to die. I, too, have seen
my image and wanted to fall into it.

Say the heart is an ungodly machine.
Say the bell breaks inside the bone clock.

No matter what the music tells me, I can't
return the beginning. I was never there.

Say the body is a needful animal petitioning the sky
to satisfy its thirst. Say it is a haunted cabinet.

A voice lives in me that is not mine. It calls
and the ground changes at its beckoning,

the road lengthens, the stone in my hand
becomes a skull I lower into a well and drink.

Gnostic Fugue

A prophet says you will be resurrected
and then you will die.

The villagers' lost children
are found in the city, flies laying eggs

in the nests of their ears.
After the burial, two soldiers make love

against the wall between the old ruin
and the new. But this is their rapture, not yours.

You are the doubter and the doubt,
worshipping a book you can't read.

The awful quiet in your heart
is not the peace you were promised,

not the trembling hush before a revelation,
not a prelude to an earthquake,

not God's silence, but his breathlessness.

The Revisionist Gospel

One of my sisters confuses gunfire with the voice of God. She
will tell you the book can be decoded. It will reveal where the
priests of resurrection hide keys to the armory where you can
purchase your choice of oblivion. The story is about a warship,
disarmed in the desert waiting for the flood when, suddenly, rain.

One of my sisters will tell you that in order to love you must
humiliate yourself. She will start the story with a virgin whose
hair is black as the bottom of the sea. In her version of the book,
the heroine worships a quixotic knight who doesn't adore her, but
who wants to release the captive lyrebird in her room. Jealousy
marshals fevered blood through her body so she finds a windmill,
which is love disguised, and sets it on fire, which is a prayer for
the damned.

One sister believes God is a guillotine, and love is an oubliette.
She knows pain is a condition of truth, and that a fossil leaves
two stories—one about unmiraculous fish and loaves and a hill
crowded with atheists muttering mass, and one about carbon.
She'll tell you the book is about a chariot dragging its charioteer
to his death. It's about what the dying man cried out for as
the earth broke his body open, and the people left behind who
worshipped the stones he bled on.

To My Unborn Daughter

They will try to make you read it, the book of plagues,
written by the dangerous one behind the stars. Do not

believe their dusty proverbs. I am a good woman.
They'll tell you we are banished, but this isn't exile.

It's a refuge from a nation of titans. Know that a man
does not have to be bigger than the tower he builds,

but a battlefield must be wider than the bodies below it.
This is yours—this cup of rain we pass as we sing.

This is yours also—what a man will do for a woman.
He will lay her in sage and empty his spurred heart

into her mouth. She will listen with her body until
he is relieved, the way the moon is relieved

when it tells its secrets to water by lying down on it.
I've never met a man without demons. Not the priest

with his scourge, nor the sailor who believes dead whales
lashed to the ship speak to him as he sharpens harpoons.

Not even the blacksmith who came home to find his wife
dead, and then beat her for leaving him. How can I

convince you that this is love? Is it luckier to have a redeemer
who will kill for you? One who will die for you?

Or one who will use your flesh to quiet his burning cigarette?
Stranger inside me, when you are born, I will give you

a closed book and ask you to never read it, never rest,
never forgive a man who wants to save you.

Become the Lion

We keep my sister alive by force,
pin her down and nurse her with raw
eggs from the chickens that did not drown

and milk taken from a goat staked
to the ground. The dull tolling of the bell
around her neck speaks as she moves.

Here, I am here. She wanders to the river,
and we find her. In a tree, singing
to a starling, we find her. We dig a grave

for the missing body, but nothing
consoles her. In mourning, the cure
is the sickness. A year ago, a lion

took our mother as she tended the fire.
This hunger bewilders me. We found half
of her bones and buried her

uneaten heart in a dead cub's rib cage.
When we returned three days later
we saw no bones, no heart, only tracks

in the sand leading east. *Ghost me. Fossil me.*
Resurrect me near dawn. We're always at the mercy
of one menacing grace, one rite, an art

that makes us suffer twice. At night we wait
with our knives where the tall grass begins.
We will kill it or die or become the lion.

Inheritance

The angel present at my birth is not
the one who attends me now, as I deliver
strange daughters I will leave in the woods

for the wolves with their names written
on their wrists—each born without breath
or a tongue, each changeling abandoned

in a thicket where aspens quake with the old
ecclesiastical terror, and blackberries still red
on the branch ripen into their second birth.

Auto-da-Fé

There is nothing left for us
in this house abandoned to scavengers

and broken hinges. Paint blisters walls,
frost crewels the windows.

In the locked hutch, newly hatched
maggots feast on dead rabbits.

Our mother is not here, but we bury
what remains of her, a bracelet of teeth

and letters addressed to no one.
The first says, *I've imprisoned God*

in my body, the whole kingdom.
We are sorry we could not be the ones

to kill her, so we lift empty bowls
and drink to blunt our grief.

Our skin creaks like ice when the river
moves under it. Underneath the bed

we hear the shadows of our mother's voice
sing when she means to weep

and weep when she means to say
she knows love will fail us.

We set fire to the house and walk out
with God's thousand names on our flesh.

To Poison the Lion

Damn the barren apple tree. Damn this hour
bruised by owls, the meteors interrupting the sky.

The organ plays its own requiem
as angels crawl the walls of the cathedral

trying to get back in. *Take my sorrow*, I beg,
but there is only one sadness here.

It is the most vulnerable part of the trinity,
and the most abiding. When a cyclone touched

the earth and offered paradise to those
who would enter, I sought the lion's den.

The knife in my hand wanted to be dangerous.
Smoke wanted to hold the burning city's silhouette

but surrendered it to the wind. I poisoned myself
to poison the lion, but when I arrived, it was dead.

Vultures tugged at its ribs with nervous bravery.
The changing body hummed its clumsy music.

Hysteria: A Requiem

Kyrie

After the plague
    we put away our lamentation,
                our children's cradles,
      and dance with all the required ecstasy.

The monks follow us with brooms, barefoot.
    The doctors in the next room
                heal each other.

      A woman in a mask leads the midwife
by a leash through the rooms.
             Behind her hood she warns,
    A nation has ended, but the world continues,
      jubilant and unclean.

Outside, spring continues without us.

      We loved a god we didn't believe in,
and believed in a god we didn't love,
      but neither let our children live.

Through cracks in the boarded windows, I see broken rocking
horses in the streets. I hear nothing. Nothing. Not even the wind.
I want to go through the houses and search for the living, but I
am bound to the known. A sore rises on my scalp. I tell no one.
The test of faith is not death but fear.

Dies Irae

No one wants to remember
    how we found bodies in trees and left them
  unburied in the sky.

On ruined carpets we wallow with pomegranates and sweet wine.
  We want to forget the wayfarer we hung
    when he asked for food.

      The truffles and caviar are ours.
  And the figs. The rosemary butter and ginger tea.
  The killdeer singing in the wet grass.

We aren't good with memories, but we are serious
    about pleasure.
  About arias and cinnamon.

      Harps and honey.

I met my love at the gallows where his father taught him to tie
a noose. He lashed his wrists to mine. We tried to burn every
cathedral in the country. Each time the stones bewildered us, so
we traveled to the forest of the damned to baptize the trees. We
wanted to become shadowless, like the sea, but the darkness that
followed us shared our names.

Offertory

The feral cats cry in estrous
        followed by nurses with a cautious hope.

     They unearth the placentas under the stairs,
          but the kittens are born
                    bathed in flame.
        Their mothers eat their fevers
            as we intone our cold hallelujahs.

We want to believe laughter will return to us.
     We make our hearts
            hosts for immortal breath.
        Mortify our flesh,
          we plead
    to the whips in our hands.

The bread does not promise to transform us,
       but the flaming sword above our heads
         threatens to forgive us.

———————————————

I rode the sea as a child, learned the names of every monster that
approached the ship, watched sharks feast on what remained of a
whale while her calf circled.

Sanctus

We strip the midwife to prove her body is
      like ours.
                  At night we tie her to
beams in the ceiling.
        Bent under her spirit's arousal
           she accuses us
                even as we sever her tongue—

      How can you say my prayers?

      How dare you say the dead child
               in my room is your son?

      This is my devotion to the returning dead.
    These are the ruins
           I mapped onto my body so I might always be lost.

I lived past the day I was told I would die. The earth didn't
rupture. The sky didn't open. I am old enough now to know we
only love what will die for us. I don't want to be forgiven for the
stories I told; I want to forget the bloodied yolk inside the broken
egg. I am responsible to what I have witnessed. I have eaten the
eyes of the enemy, and I am the enemy.

Agnus Dei

We steal an hour from the future and burn
   all the books so history begins with us.

  We write:
      In the beginning light begat shadow,
  flowers begat fruit,
       but stars were fatherless.
  The wheat, radiant and unkind.

  We grow bored with paradise
    and take down the old commandments,
     but can't write new ones.

We sell each other stories of happiness
       but the pages are blank.

     The starling starts to charge for its song,
   its nest heavy with copper coins.

I know nothing of my father's myths, but my mother's parables
are sewn into my skirt. She gave me tarnished idols and her long
shadow. I come from a line of obedient women who want me to
believe only the strong lie under the stones they're given, but I am
not buried under the cairn. I am smearing blood on the lintels
even though the angel already passed over.

Lux aeterna

Now, in the last world, we bury nightingales
               beneath the floor.
       Trackers with their ears to the ground listen
            for angels approaching.

Where is the saint,   mortally torn and wearing a hood of stars,
      bearing her own redemption?

      Rumors make women rush
           with tributes of roasted songbirds
                        to the fallen temples,
           but the epidemic continues.
               We remain empty.

Before they left
               priests tied laws to our wrists that said:
     Grief is a slow animal
            bearing an imperfect hope.

I try to name this feeling. This terrible lightness others call
peace. I felt it once, watching bare trees, waiting for wary deer to
approach the salt. Nothing sang. Bears gave birth in their sleep,
and the cubs crawled out to admire their indigo shadows in
the snow.

Libera me

The doctors name our malady—
                    Hysteria: suffering of the womb.

We want to be healed,
                    relieved of our burden,
          so we remake our children   with clay, sing them
                    lullabies and offer our breasts
                              with the hesitation of new brides.

     We let waves
                    rock them past the shoals,
                              set fire to our dresses
                                        to transform ourselves
                    into the ashes that pursue them across the sea.

———————————————————

I gave birth to a daughter, denied her three times, and when I
found her at the ocean's edge, I wound her in a sheet and offered
her to the man who walked toward me on the water.

Somniloquy

In the end, everything matters,
even rain on the hills, though it won't
save a splintered boat from sundering

or release the shark in the net.
Bathing my sick child in milk couldn't
calm her fever. Nailing myself to a tree

didn't bring God any closer,
but when I looked a serpent in the eyes
I felt a common salvation.

•

The day after I buried my daughter
I heard knocking and opened a drawer
to find a dozen eggs, one of them rocking.

I held it in my mouth. Two snakes broke
from the shell and licked my neck. The god
hanging on the wall commanded, *Watch me suffer.*

•

I dreamt my daughter dove
for whale bones on the abyssal plains,
surfaced from the seafloor bearing

spines, ribs, colossal skulls.
They grinned at me from the waves,
gods of a different history.

•

Two days after I buried my daughter
I began to understand I was promised
a second life but not a better one.

I hired mourners who wept and rent their clothes
by the river, but visions still pursued me.
I paid a woman to baptize herself in my name,

to tell me when she changed. She disappeared
but left behind a white dress and three teeth.
A woman's body is a memory with no language.

•

I dreamt my daughter by the side of the road
circled by thirteen dead owls. I knew it
would end here in the cat's cradle of my heart,

in my witch's little finger, but my daughter said,
Be still. It has not been decided whether you will die
on this dark continent or the next.

•

Three days after I buried my daughter,
I found a man in a field holding the soft, gray
loops of his intestines in his hands like evidence

of life, but not proof. I killed the bull
that gored him, stitched its head
onto the dead man's body. When I saw

what I had made, I kissed its nipples,
drank there until I was strong enough
to brush the flies from my breasts.

The Sunken Gospel

The sea is thirsty and the shadow of a whale
moves below the ship, angry at anchors, harpoons,
the weathered breasts of the mermaid on the bow.

Sailors on deck strip the flesh to find the fat.
They sever the head and drain the oil. All night
their hands on their faces. Not from shame. No.

There are blood blisters on their palms, but their wrists
smell like women. As it dies, the whale hears its mother
singing a mile away, two fathoms deep.

Now for the ruthless season. Now for the dreams rising
out of the whale's split heart, moaning blue zodiac hymns
to the sleepers. There are three canals in the ear,

two windows, one voice from the beautiful dead.
One omega anthem. One mind editing between hammerfalls,
the promise of a devout music and a common enemy.

The lights turn away as the men turn in their hammocks,
their hearts translating the sunken gospel,
wondering if they hear women singing green valentines

in the water or deaf angels chanting before the war.
Tomorrow they'll kill the birds because there's too much music.
Tomorrow they'll wake with dirt in their hands.

Dance, *Glory*

On the backs of dead sailors we drift the treasonous sea,
naming constellations of amputated saints, stars riddling

their bodies with bright wounds. Our blood is wherever
we taste it. We lick the knives clean. There is no paradise

waiting for us, so why ask for miracles? The gods listen
but never lead rain to the fire. We could ask waves

not to erase us. We could praise the prodigal moon
and plead for high tide. If we wanted to survive,

we could beg the storm to forgive the captain
who branded us with the ship's name, who ordered us

to dance, *Glory* blackening our thighs, who sang
to the lightning as he swept ashes from his burning ship.

Parable of the Cannibals

When we undressed him we saw the veins in his feet. But before we tasted the sixteen muscles of his tongue, before we chained his vagrant heart to the anchor, our faces blackened with hunger, we baited our hooks with darkness.

Before our bodies grew weak from salt and dread, we rode the tempest, lanced by wind, pursued by thunder and the sound of the mast splintering. We were terrified of the sea's power, but the thunder was the sermon and not the truth.

When we boarded the ship we thought there was no reason to be afraid—all the witches had been hung. We promised each other the difficult work of love, which is one part yes, two parts joy and three parts forgiveness. We sold the gold in our teeth to pay for passage. As we walked to the docks, mud burrowed into the cracked soles of our boots and the slaughterhouse gleamed with rain.

Dirge for the Idol

I drank from your mouth, and look at what
has become of me. I made a feast for you,
but locusts broke from your throat and covered

the orchard. I sought you in the sea, rowed
over the ocean's deep meridian
and dreamt a deluge for thirty nights.

I followed the blood to its source
and found my own pierced hands.
I looked for you in a forest but came upon

young foxes teething on their mother's body.
I ignored the scholar afraid of music
and the mystic afraid of laughter

and listened instead to the wisdom
of madness. I went to see the man
whose teeth grow as the moon waxes

and helped the complicit asylum guards
bait him with dead rabbits and white-throated girls.
I learned that humans love the spectacle

of suffering, but never learned why.
I learned the power that keeps us
on earth is invisible, the force turning

the world's axis, unseen. And you would have me
love your image. All my life my eyes sought
nothing but what would please my heart

to possess. You see nothing but the offerings
at your feet, flowers in the fullest diameter
of their blossoming, the slain ram's blood hardening,

arcane darkness in his open eye.
And so, bright eidolon, I will bury you
like I buried all my enemies. When I find you

made of gold, I will melt you into a coin.
Your silver statues will become rings
for young brides. Because I am angry

the apple never atones for its beauty.
Because when I stitched my eyelids open
and looked at the sun, I felt the unmerciful fire.

Petition

In the temple, a pear blackens in a statue's palm.
Birds steal the grain. A man climbs the steps
holding his severed hand, but no miracle occurs.

His body refuses to reach out and claim what it lost.
A woman in a white dress waits to be overshadowed
as she plucks her eyelashes—one for the horses,

one for the rain, one for the hair on the back
of her lover's hands. She wants her virtue
restored, to return to a morning when her skin

was new and unwounded, when her mouth still fit
her mother's breast. You came to ask if it's true,
if angels weep until their faces become human,

and if the dead can escape their tombs, then—
You trap wind as it enters the statue's mouth,
and command it to rise, walk.

Our Lady of the Ruins

We exhausted ourselves
    with every available pleasure,
tied ourselves to chairs,
        naked and disobedient.

                Their bodies dusted
                with the sex of flowers

Inside our bodies, it was night.
        God knew what we asked for   *it is the bees that call me*
    but would not return our shame.

                from the bottom
One day the walls wept your image.   *of the lake*
    When we painted over it,
        your face bled through,
appeared to us in the image of our mother,   *No one remembers me*
        but penitent, adoring.   *not even   the rain*

You should know we are guilty.
        We raised more demons   *Once, before I was named*
than we could lay down.   *I lived as a woman*
        So what if we're haunted.
        So what if we've stopped dreaming.

                Nothing followed me

We are sensitive to the tides
    and the lighthouse burning
for ships that never arrive.   *I could name every plant*

The rumors are true.   Delirium found us.

knew the weather
before it announced itself

We oiled and kissed a stranger's burnt feet.
        We held pigeons under water
    until their gnarled hearts stopped
        fluttering in our hands.

My hands picked peaches
kneaded dough
dug in fresh black earth

    When we unwound their intestines
        looking for the message,
we found   blood,   hollow bones.

Now they push mushrooms
through the loam
beneath a fox's skull

Don't tell us we're too late.
        We swear we're not saved.

Now they lead ants
    to the dead mouse

We are ravished and unclean.
We left blood in the bowl for you
        and the tips of our fingers.

I was vanishing
but now I return

We forsake the eastern star.
    Take us by the hair.
                Lead us past
the ignorant light,
        past a God who threatens
            to love all that we are.

In a dress sewn
from my shroud

I will meet you
where the cross burns

Winter Nocturne

We wait for the moon to rise so we can enter
the woods and hang statues of saints from the trees.

In a thicket, a doe bent in what could be prayer
nudges her young, waiting for it to rise

from its cold sleep. Owls listen for mice beneath
the snow. The messenger of the gods is also a god.

We carry the dead fawn to the frozen pond,
and in spring it disappears. The ice weakens,

water hides the body. Nothing will hurt us
like love, not even the deer that follows us when

we return to collect the unbroken saints, last season's
nests cradled between branches, all of them empty.

The Blessing

No one wants to take the stillborn robin
curled in its blue egg, caught

between dreaming and its first morning,
and put it back in its mother's nest.

No one wants to be the one to put their hand
in the lion's mouth. It waits beyond the fire.

Something always waits beyond the fire—
not a bride, but a white dress. Not a foal,

but its bones. Something waits inside a black tent
in a yellowed field—an archangel with two hearts

in his chest. When he asks for a sacrifice, I offer
another woman's son. The blood on my hands

becomes wine. No one wants to claim the child
bathed in flame, turning its new body toward the trees.

Requiem for the Firstborn

Before the sandstorm in the bell tower,
but after a child covers her ears to make the silence
louder, you will find my story in the book of fires.

Here, where all love ends, in a house
that is no longer a house, where I found the devil
on the stairs. I put my head in his lap and cried,

Deceive me, O ruined angel. Once, I had to choose
between an honest widow and a lying orphan,
and I chose the coyote nailed to the fence.

Once, I thought the wound was a mouth,
so I kissed it. And the devil said, *Why are you afraid?*
A good fear is useful if you find a changeling

left out in the wilderness to die. I tried to touch his face,
but he had no face, so I kissed his burnt eyelids.
The devil said, *There's no use lying to the dead.*

They have no more need for beauty. But I need. I lie.
I mean everything I never say. Sometimes I confuse
my fears with the names of my children.

Sometimes the name I cry into the darkness
is my own. With the garden on my left
and the singing bones to my right, where can I go?

If the lamb tugs milk from its mother's body, then
I can take my hand out of the lion's mouth.
If night forgives the sun its eagerness,

I can burn down the sugar cane, I can take down
the plantation brick by burning brick, I can fill in
the dry well where I hear a child crying.

How to Find the Underworld

Enter the serpent's mouth, and sadness will walk
in you like a pilgrim through the desert.
The descent feels something like your devotion

to empty rooms, and something like a ladder.
There are demons, of course, and stone owls
on the entrance to frighten away crows.

If you go deep enough you will recognize the dead
by their sins. Hornets and forsaken children attend them.
Be careful. Your heart will testify against itself.

The daughter who approaches you is not the one
you lost. The quarantined infants rocked in cradles
made from the twisted rib cages of horses

do not hold her either. I would spare you anything
but this—her first word was for her father,
and her last was one of God's names.

You can't bring her back. You can't bring back
anything from here that you want to keep. Only grief
and a new obedience and four pounds of ash.

Stillborn Elegy

We can't remember her name, but we remember where
we buried her. In a blanket the color of a sky that refuses birds.

The illiterate owls interrogate us from the trees, and we answer,
We don't know. Maybe we named her Dolores, for our grandmother,

meaning sadness, meaning the mild kisses of a priest.
Maybe we called her Ruth, after the missionary who gave us

a rifle and counterfeit wine. We blindfolded our sister and tied
her hands because she groped the fence looking for the rabid fox

we nailed to a post. Katydids sang with insistent summer urge
and the cavalier moon grew more slender. In the coyote hour,

we offered benedictions for a child we may have named Aja,
meaning unborn, meaning the stillness that entered us,

which is the stillness inside the burnt piano, which is also
the woman we untie, who is the mother of stillness.

Late Novena

I can't tell you where I found the lion or what it had
in its mouth, but I can tell you all the old stories
are about sacrifice, like the beggar who chained

church bells around the neck of a lamb and offered it
to the river. I can tell you the old secrets—
how an albatross found the ocean floor but had to die

to reach it, or how the soul is exiled to the body,
the body an interruption between shadow and light.
I can whisper that an army buried in the desert will rise again

when the sun dies, or tell you the force tugging
planets toward a star is called longing. A black hole
is called beautiful. I tell you a word's sharp edge

can split the stitches binding your unrepentant lips.
Come back. Tell us what you've seen. Tell us
you met a god so reckless, so lonely, it will love us all.

Envoi

You said abundance would not harm me,
but none of your songs could stop

the god-awful fullness of the moon.
Even the plague ended in feast,

birds chirping fat and happy
in their nests. I tried other oceans,

climbed a volcano to look inside
the earth, walked to the edge

of the sinkhole that swallowed a city.
My freedom only made me more afraid.

I'm not sure there is any world
but this one, and the mango's sweetness

is terrible to me. Some days fire is a mirror.
Some days I can bear the stillness of elk

when I surprise them in the alder.
Yesterday I cleaned bones out of the boat

and met a child on shore. He made a gun
out of his hand. No one taught him this.

He raised his arm, fingers leveled
at my heart. You said I could contain it,

this gift. The boy told me I could keep
the boat. The bones were his.

Come Trembling

In the country where believers eat the bodies
of the gods, we meet a priest who pulls a rope
of thorns through his tongue to make his mind

pure enough for a vision. He dances to music
we can't hear and waits to come trembling
into knowledge. We don't recognize ourselves

in his radiance, but we do in his suffering.
He passes through pain and into healing
without seeing the holy rendered visible.

He tells us the oracle died when she refused
to divine the future, but we find her tangled
in her own hair wearing a garland of burrs,

manacled to the bed. We ask for a better world
to die in, but she says, *Submit to your freedom.*
We tie new knots in her hair and swim

into the belly of a shark to retrieve the book
of signs. Rumors say the secret of life is sewn
into a dead man's coat, but when we unearth him,

all we find in his sleeves are his fractured arms.
We want to believe, to split open the myth
and lie in it, return to original dark and be changed,

but the bones won't yield to us, pages are missing
from the book, the gods remain so quiet
we hear water speaking between the stones.

The Orchard of Infinite Pears

On a mountain, we find monks who won't speak
because they cannot bear the way sound travels

and returns. They take us to their cave—genesis-dark
and deep as dream—and there we read history

by the light of their bodies. The book says: *Myths*
invent nothing. And the book says: *We are all born again.*

The monks point to a nova pulsing in the eastern sky
when they mean to say creation is a sacred violence.

When they learned they were ruled by time the way
the sea is ruled by the moon, they came to the wilderness

and buried the cold machinery of clocks, the arms
and wheels and chimes that signified their dying.

They grew an orchard of pears to escape the mysteries,
to take solace in the wonted work of sow and reap.

Here they could feel the heft of a harvest in their pockets,
count seeds and the fruit they bore, recording the measurable

world. But then they cut a pear in half, and halved it again,
and again halved it. They divided it by zero and have not

stopped counting, trees slivered away by arithmetic.
What is zero, but an elegy? we ask. *We are afraid of everything*

we cannot touch, they write, notching bark with a number
that continues unsolved—ordinary and divine and forever.

Parable of Love's Twelve Apostles

You can find one in the arsonist who collects boxes of burnt matches. One in the parishioners who stick their hands in coat pockets, pricking their fingers on splinters of a crucifix. Another joins the crowd with closed eyes and raised hands trying to reach a sacred statue. Another sleeps in the statue that collapses on those who worship it.

Others hide in the scars on a horse's back. They shake pagan trees as their roots seek a darker earth. They crawl inside caskets piled with roses and into the winter carolers refuting grief. One is in the song that tells a slave how to escape. The ground sings, *This way.* The heart says, *Follow it.*

You can also find one with the man in his room painting a sparrow he killed so he might see the divine specifics of feather, beak, wing. One even smiles on the stage where a woman is bound and the crowd cries out for her death. The exultant apostle knows love is the boy in attendance, holding his father's hand. Love is the baker selling bread to the hangman. And love is the sun in the witch's hair.

The Shepherd of Lesser Gods

Every day we wake to a new god and devour
an old vision. We make the forbidden visible

when we fill thimbles on the windowsill
with holy water. Ghosts enter the rooms

before we do, parading their practical immortality.
Nothing surprises us, not even our own salvation.

Not even waking to a weeping madonna by our beds
lamenting that god is chained to the men who made him.

We can't remember sleeping, but we remember
our dreams. The shepherd of lesser gods tells us

bread is still mistaken for a missing body,
and a missing body is still mistaken for a miracle.

We look for you. Chart maps, but the landscape
changes as we travel over it. Our shadows

lengthen. We find thorns in our hair, but never
a shroud. We hear you are at the market

buying images of yourself, but when we arrive,
we only see the dead hunting for their ashes.

Sans Terre

Those who have heard continents drifting
from each other must offer orisons to the god

of maladies and reluctant miracles.
Prophets take skeletons from catacombs

so they can declare Rapture while night hides
our shadows from us. We discover keys

in our pockets, but never the doors they belong to.
When we leave a thimble, a bullet, and a pearl

by the fire at dusk, they're missing by dawn.
We lumber into deserts to feel our sweat cooling

into salt in the scoop of our collarbones.
We navigate the dunes by stars and sidewinders.

It's not the grail we want, but to journey toward
our longing. We want to find the tomb empty.

Reveal yourself, we whisper when we mean to say,
Refuse us the moonburnt body. Remain vast and wild

and unknown. A song lives in the robin whether it sings
or not. Therefore music. Therefore masquerade.

Therefore mourners planting ghost orchids means
they saw your wounds close as they reached to touch them.

Revelation

I sing of the statue's virgin breast,
the one I touched when no one was looking.

I sing of bats sleeping in caves, of gnats
troubling the scab over the lion's eye,

of beetles crawling into the ear of the sphinx
who stopped riddling long before the flood.

After the rapture there is more waiting.
Blood runs from walls. I can't find money

for the ransom. The man's body I pull
from beneath the bed bears no wounds except

the medals pinned to his bare chest. I sing
of the children's graveyard in a refugee camp,

and of a country with barracudas and lemon trees.
I am from the tribe named in the second chapter

of the book, and I am on my knees asking
for permission to doubt again. I sing of brothers

who crucified crows to fence posts. Their mother
died anyway. I am brave the way any fool is brave.

I sing of a sheep and the wolf at its throat,
of a goat and its clanking bell, of blood cell

and bone spur and of time which conquers both.
I sing the truth. I sing to survive it.

The New World

We see mountains first, the earth in conflict
with itself. Land of juggernauts, of mummies held
timeless in honey. We make circles around the clouds'

shadows on the ground, careless as wildflowers, reciting
minor revelations and the names of trees we've never seen.
A man builds a theater of snow and ruins it with salt.

A wild girl blunders out of the woods but returns
tearing at her dress and warbling the strange language
of foxes. Hallowed be this squandered country.

Even when we find pyrite in the streams we remain
faithful. Even when the shy wolverines come down
from the hills and carry away the paper birds,

pinned and spinning, above our beds. Still, the dark
forgives the sun its eagerness. The boy forgives the bull
that gored him. We believe because the night after

the birds were stolen, we woke up singing. We heal
whether we want to or not. Whenever we raise
our hands to the sky, they are filled with light.

Jubilee

Seven times seven years—The fiftieth year you shall make sacred. . . .

It shall be a Jubilee for you, when every one of you shall return home.

LEVITICUS 25:8–10

By now I know the miles my blood travels
each year. I know the mendicant's hunger—

hollowness moves in, my body becomes
the cave I am seeking. I drag the jaws

of a dead wolf from its den for the meat between
his teeth. I am red and reeking with the journey.

I am a ravening animal weeping for the angel
with broken hands standing sentry over the ossuary.

I am harrowed, hallowed. I am stone, stone,
I have not trembled. Love nails me to the world.

Notes

"To My Unborn Daughter"—the line "the dangerous one behind the stars" is from Rilke's *Duino Elegies,* translated by A. Poulin Jr.

"Gnostic Fugue"—the line "I am the doubter and the doubt" is from Ralph Waldo Emerson's *Brahma.*

"Parable of the Cannibals"—the line "baited my hook with darkness" is modified from Henry David Thoreau's *Walden Pond.*